# ELSIE'S VOICE

*Karen Chambers*

**BALBOA**.PRESS
A DIVISION OF HAY HOUSE

Balboa Press books may be ordered through booksellers or by contacting:

Balboa Press
A Division of Hay House
1663 Liberty Drive
Bloomington, IN 47403
www.balboapress.com.au
AU TFN: 1 800 844 925 (Toll Free inside Australia)
AU Local: (02) 8310 7086 (+61 2 8310 7086 from outside Australia)

Print information available on the last page.

ISBN: 978-1-9822-9453-3 (sc)
ISBN: 978-1-9822-9454-0 (e)

Balboa Press rev. date: 07/20/2022

# Contents

# Foreword

**This book discusses information about sexual assault which may triggering to a survivor.

A long time ago I lost something very precious to me...my inner child. I had no idea how important connecting to her would be. I had separated from her a long time ago. In my mind these memories belonged to someone else....Elsie.

When writing about my experience with suppressed memories, I realised how fragile the mind can become. It was only after learning to navigate the subconscious and the conscious mind to work in harmony that I was going to gain any sense of peace.

When reaching out for help or studies on repressed memories, I was greeted with the fact it is controversial. This subject is a 'Hot Potato'. There is an assumption that most people want retribution, but what they really want is peace and to be heard. It is not about blame, it's about awareness.

When I was 47 years old, I received flashes of a memory from when I was very young. 3 years old in fact. Working through the shock of accessing these memories would become one of the darkest periods of my life. When one of the full memories came to me, I wrote it down. I was worried about losing the memory again. I sealed it in an envelope and put it in a drawer. I have no desire to read the envelope again, but I am grateful I preserved the memory. It was not about what happened. It was about how it affected my life. The realisation of what had happened at such a young age was very disturbing. I could not fathom something like that could happen to me. Even though I had a lot of anxiety growing up I had a very happy childhood. Realising the truth, I separated my inner child from myself. This must have happened to someone else. I called the little girl Elsie. (Someone Else)

# A Meeting of the Minds

I always knew something felt different. I didn't quite fit. I didn't know why, but I knew something inside was suffocating me. I'm not sure how old Elsie was when I met her. She had tried to introduce herself to me a few times, but I was too busy trying to fend off the alligators that had crept up in the swamp I had created in my life.

I didn't realise she was trying to help me. She was trying to relieve the inner turmoil that I had accumulated. I was scared of her. Was it her fault that my life ended up like this? If she was stronger maybe her voice would have protected me. Protected my children from the shambles of a life I had managed to create. Part of me felt bad for her and part of me wished she didn't exist. Why was she born so innocent and trusting? From the moment Elsie came into this world she was full of curiosity and gratitude. She delighted in other people's happiness and felt most at peace when she could sit and just take in the world and the people in it. I often wonder if it was really the right time for Elsie to come to me. She had good intentions, but was never on quite the same wave length as everyone else around her. I don't believe anything in life is a mistake, so people can't be mistakes either. I am truly grateful for everyone who has been a part of my life They have all given me insights, life lessons and journeys of self-discovery.

Elsie was very intense to me as she represented fear in the rawest form. She also represented truth and authenticity and I knew once I opened the door to her there was no turning back. At times it was easier to ignore her and deny my own truth. The inherent fear of the unknown journey ahead would keep me locked in denial. Letting her in was going to be the scariest thing I have ever done. Judgements, doubts and declining mental health; it was all about to flood in. There was never going to be a right time. Besides it was her timing and agenda not mine. Her intentions for me were always to have my best interests at heart. She had no choice but to love me and want the best for me. Even so, sometimes when showing the best parts of yourself it is also necessary to show the worst parts of yourself. It is called being authentic.

One of the biggest barriers to becoming authentic is shame and fear is a part of shame. It is the fear of being disconnected to others and being misunderstood which keeps us locked in shame. Learning how to show our vulnerability leads us to connection with others. Being vulnerable requires us to show our real truth and let go of the fear. (Brown, 2010)

However, being vulnerable also means exposing yourself to ridicule and judgement. Getting to the raw self and stripping back to the true identity. No masks, no coaching, no makeup, no hiding. Is there ever going to be a right time for exposing your own truth?

# Carrying the Burdens of Others

"I can't deal with you now. Everything is crashing in on me. I don't have the strength to hear your voice."

I was depleted of emotional energy and dealing with situations beyond what I ever thought I was capable of dealing with. I didn't think I could get out of all this mess a whole person. I also didn't realise I was starting to fall into a trap of anxiety and panic attacks. On the outside I coped and knew I was capable. On the inside I questioned every fibre of my capability and sanity. Why was life for me and my family so dysfunctional?

All I ever wanted to do was help people. I didn't realise I was not in the position to help others. I truly thought I was. I was not capable of carrying the burdens of others as well as my own. I'm not sure if there was anyone that was capable of carrying the burden of some of the people around me that needed it. Some situations can be pretty challenging and during this time Elsie came to visit me often. My world became very dark, very quickly. At times I definitely felt like I was losing grip on reality.

I was two people. There was the capable, intelligent, funny, likeable Karen. Then there was the sad, anxious, terrified, angry Karen. There was a volcano of anger inside me, and I didn't know what put it there. I knew Elsie had shown me. I guessed she showed me for my own good and wellbeing, but I didn't like being exposed to it. I wanted to get on with my life and tapping into the anger was debilitating. Hadn't I already been through enough? Why did I have to keep finding emotional strength when I had already battled my fair share of wars.

I knew who the real Karen was. I knew she was likeable. I knew people gravitated to her. So why was there someone else inside me that came out and ruined situations for me? Why did she have to exist?

I remember someone telling me once that it was like I had layers of cement inside me. I had been able to crumble some layers, but I still had some to go. That is exactly how it felt for me. Just when I felt like I was breaking through my emotional walls I found more layers of cement. In 2012 I studied at a university and did a small study on childhood memories and the subconscious. It fascinated me as Elsie had shown herself to me the year before. The subconscious seems to have this way of protecting us from memories that may be too much. I have not really been able to find that much more research on the subconscious since then.

The strange thing to me is if the subconscious guards painful memories to protect us, then why do we get the memories back later on? Why not just stay there buried and safe, locked away to leave us in peace? And if we are shown these memories why not give us the whole story. It is a difficult thing to understand. Humans are only just starting to be able to remember things at around three years and not fully able to till around 7 years old. Carole Peterson from The University of Newfoundland called it Childhood amnesia. (Peterson,2017)

Repressed memories are a very cruel experience to have. I always said mental illness is very unkind as the people around the person who is suffering cannot see inside the brain and see it is sick. We can see a broken leg or the effects of terrible disease, but we cannot understand the depth of empathy and support needed for someone unwell with mental illness. Repressed memories are also a merciless experience as we can't quite grab onto the memory. However, we still feel all the effects and fears the same way as if we remembered every detail. It feels like you are reaching out to grab the answers you have waited for and then they are taken away just as you touch them.

The ironic thing for me is that I now access my subconscious a lot more through meditation. I am constantly trying to understand the balance between the conscious and subconscious. Humans function in a state of consciousness, but most of us are still curious about the level that the subconscious can access dreams and what some would call our higher self or soul.

Me as a toddler

# Dreams

Are the dreams your fault or mine Elsie? I never understood why I kept getting these dreams. They were exhausting, especially the ones where I couldn't get home. I could see home in the distance, but just as I got closer it always moved further away. I also had many dreams of blocked toilets or being exposed while going to the toilet. These dreams were again exhausting as it seemed like I was never getting relief. I don't get these dreams as much, but every now and then I will get one. Were these dreams your fault or mine Elsie? As I began to interpret the dreams the memories became more important to me. Somehow, I needed closure.

I went to hypnotherapy to see if I could get some answers, but that just gave me more questions than answers. The first hypnotherapist I went to was very clinical and abrupt. He seemed disinterested. He was never going to get anything out of me. Neither of us knew exactly what I was looking for. When I came home from my first session, I felt an overwhelming sense of grief. I truly felt like I had lost something. I didn't know what it was. I went to the beach and tried to tap into that grief and wrote about loss. For me it felt like the loss of who I was supposed to be as a child.

I was desperate for answers so I could give Elsie some peace. I wasn't progressing very far, and my anger was not subsiding. I was also taking on some family issues I just wasn't equipped for. I felt like I was starting to lose my mind. The more I tried to explain the more peculiar my behaviour became. I was getting nowhere so I had to tell Elsie to be quiet. *I couldn't help her.*

A few years later I was steered to hypnotherapy again and it was a much better experience. She was a lovely person who took the time and patience to break through. She also referred me to a psychologist. I felt very alone during this period. The only person who truly understood what I was going through was my therapist. I went to see her regularly for two and a half years. She knew how I was going to feel before I did. It meant so much to me to have someone who didn't think I was making all this up. Not only did she believe me, but she also predicted my behaviours. I remember the first session she described my life for me. I was so shocked. It actually made me feel somewhat normal. She assured me she had sat across many Karen's in her years as a psychologist.

Going to therapy opened me up. There was way more inside me that I understood. I thought I would go for three months, get fixed and have a good life. Boy was I wrong. Therapy was just the start. Now the wound was open, and it was getting infected by some of the broken personalities I had to deal with at the time. Thinking back, I didn't realise how close I was to the edge. I started having panic attacks. I had never experienced them before. Previously another therapist told me I had been displaying symptoms of Post-Traumatic Stress during the sessions at times.

I remember as a teenager struggling with my body trembling and my throat closing over. I never knew what was going to trigger it. I just knew that as soon as I got blotches on my neck I was about to shake. This was extremely embarrassing and not the look of the cool teenager I wanted to be. Like most teenagers I felt extremely awkward most of the time. However, I had the added awkwardness of Post-Traumatic Stress symptoms that were never kind or understanding. These symptoms called the shots and they decided at what times to show up. When I was going through this, I was totally unaware that I was experiencing PTSD symptoms.

Coming out of denial was going to be quite a process for me. I'm not sure I am out of denial yet. For me, opening up about what I had been going through made me very vulnerable. Connecting to other people meant I was willing to expose the most personal side of myself. Exposure to me is an extremely uncomfortable state. Maybe there is some 'Freudian' explanation there.

As I started to become more vulnerable, I felt my confidence plummet. I was delving right inside. Many times I felt like I was losing control. If I lost control, then fear could rule me. I just couldn't allow that. I had to keep fighting.

One particular dream I had I called 'Facing my Fears.' It was longwinded as dreams are, but at the end I was alone in a dark house and a scary ghostly figure came straight up to me and stood in front of me. I was terrified, but I got the message it was time to face my fears and to stare it down. The longer I stood staring at this figure the less scary they became to me.

For me to face my fears I had to find out what they were. I wanted to be strong. I wanted to be seen as a strong woman. I was more than capable of that. So, what is something I could do to show people how brave I really was ...... I could jump out of a plane!

So, on the 10th of August 2014 I jumped out of a perfectly good plane at 14000 feet.

There now that shows everyone. That took a lot of guts. I can just get on with my life now. I had done a bungee jump when I was 35, surely jumping out of a plane topped that. I thought acting brave would conquer my fears, but it was just that— 'acting'. I had avoided facing my fears for a very long time. Deep down I knew this was going to be a scary process. I had two choices. Heal the wound or learn to live with it. The problem was the wound was buried under layers of cement. I had learnt to go around the cement rather than penetrate through it. When I made the decision to crush the cement and breakthrough, I knew there was no turning back. It was going to be a bumpy ride and probably pretty ugly.

# Connection

I deserved peace. I knew I had made some questionable choices in my life, but I still deserved peace. I was also a very intelligent, compassionate woman and had a lot to give to this world. Some of the choices I made in my life made me feel like I was stupid. A smart person would not make bad choices. Over this journey I realised there are no bad choices in life. There are experiences and lessons. Good bad and in-between. However, I truly believe everything happens for a reason. Embracing your personal journey is what makes us all unique. Facing what was ahead was going to be rough, but the outcome would be worth it. I wanted to live an honest life. In fact, I didn't think I could pretend anymore. Authenticity was important for me. I had to feel real so I could connect. That word again 'connection'.

"Who is that? Stop it. I'm tired of this. Who keeps punching me in the face?" Every time I tried to see who it was I couldn't see their face. As I started to open up to facing the truth I finally saw who was punching me in the face. It was me. I heard a voice whisper to me. "Stop beating yourself up Karen." These dreams were also exhausting, but I don't seem to get them anymore. As my recurring dreams dissipated Elsie was not around as much. As I write this, I'm not sure where she is. I know she is not gone. I started this process for her. She deserved to be heard. She may have grown into a completely different person if she had allowed herself to be heard. If someone had listened, she may have thrived and become a confident strong woman instead of staying a young child.

# Far from Nobody

Growing up I always felt different and alone. I had drawn a picture of a face on our toilet wall in our first house. I didn't get in trouble for it and I'm not sure how long it stayed before being taken off. I called the face 'Mr Nobody'. I would actually go into the toilet and talk to him. Writing this now it seems so sad, but the funny thing is I don't remember always feeling that sad growing up. I have a lot of fond memories going on holiday and playing with friends. Although I did feel disconnected a lot. Today I suppose it would be classed as depression. There is a lot more acceptance about children having trouble with anxiety and depression.

I remember once instance in primary school when I befriended a girl that would be seen as big for her age. She was very shy and definitely a lost soul as far as being noticed. Even at that age I gravitated to the loners because I knew how it felt. We were walking around at recess and a group of boys starting chanting about fat and skinny walking together. Even though I was a loner I felt so bad for her. What gave them the right to just decide to make someone feel so bad about themselves?

When you are a child who is always left alone on the playground not only do you believe you are unworthy of connection to anyone, you also become vulnerable to the less moral people in life that usually use you for their own purpose or entertainment. Today some primary schools have a bench where lonely children can sit. Then other children can go and sit next to them and make them feel that they have 'been seen'. What a wonderful idea.

Teenage years for me were very awkward. I did not realise I had an anxiety disorder. I was basically known as the quiet one. It took me a while to let anyone into my world. If you were part of my world, it meant I trusted you. I had some girlfriends who understood me and I am still friends with some today. Dating was extremely hard. I remember wondering why I acted the way I did. I joked that anyone would think something happened to me as a child. I was walking down the street with my first boyfriend and a friend, and I chose to stand on the outside of my friend and not hold his hand. I knew this was strange behaviour, but I didn't know why I was doing it. I didn't understand what was happening.

Another time at school I was getting ready for sport and had to change into a very short sports skirt. A friend of mine (didn't stay friends long), said she needed to go back to her locker to get something. She had long slender brown legs. I was extremely self-conscious in my skirt. Awkward was not the word for it. She begged me to go with her. I felt like I was almost naked. When we got to the locker there was a group of boys standing around. I wanted to dig a hole and dive in. I certainly wasn't fat, but my legs didn't compare to hers. She waltzed through the corridors like a gazelle, and I hid as best I could. I got a message back through the grapevine a few days later that I had chunky legs. When I look at the photos of that time, I didn't have fat legs at all. I think it is seen as a right for some teenagers to humiliate whoever they can for no good reason. If only they could see the lasting damage that focusing on body image has. Body image has always been an issue for me. I always felt disconnected from my body and saw it as a negative thing. I used to cover up a lot during these years. I was wondering where this loathing of body image came from. I figure that a paedophile would not abuse an important person. Important people don't get damaged. So, I must have been unimportant. It's alright to damage something that is unworthy of being important. I didn't get any help to understand afterwards either, so I just wasn't important. My body did this to me. I have struggled with self-worth most of my life. These years in my life were awkward and humiliating.

# Triggers

I started my first job when I was 15 almost 16. Even though my boss was a woman she had the exact same colour hair as the person in my repressed memories. It was a short hairstyle as well. She even had some similar features like the shape of the nose. I started to get terrible symptoms when she spoke to me directly. Even just mentioning her name was a trigger for me. As you can imagine my co-workers thought I was pretty weird. They kept asking me what was happening, and I couldn't explain it. All I knew was that I would get blotches on my chest and neck then my throat would go dry and close over. My teeth and body would shake and chatter. As soon as I felt the blotches coming, I knew what was coming and couldn't stop it. I just had to ride it out. If I could leave the room I would.

My Mother was quite concerned about these symptoms and took me to a doctor who referred me to a specialist. He said I had anxiety and would grow out of it. No investigation, no explanation why or concern for my mental health. Just she will grow out of it. Well, *I didn't*. I did learn to control my breathing, but even today I get the blotches, chattering teeth and body shaking.

I knew parts of me were Elsie. When I would get angry or frustrated, I would stamp my feet like a small child. I would feel her isolation and fear. But I was an adult and had to let her go. She was at times pretty insistent to be heard. I was the only one she could rely on to speak up for her. She lost her voice a long time ago.

# Freedom

Freedom is not a state of mind it is continual. It is a feeling. Stephen Hawkins had the freedom to do nothing else but think. His thoughts have probably changed the world in some way. He didn't have the freedom to walk or even talk, but freedom is not always what someone sees. It is what it means to the person seeking it.

I had responsibilities as a mother, partner and provider. I had to find a balance between responsibilities and freedom. I had to continually find the energy to balance the effort needed to heal while dealing with the responsibilities I had. I remember asking my therapist if she thought I was losing my mind. She told me she wouldn't let that happen. I truly believe I was very close. I had tried to contain things inside and wore many masks to show on the outside I was functioning and capable.

I woke up, I sent children off to school, went to work. I fought off phone calls and constant interruptions to my working life and just kept trying to keep steady, so I didn't succumb to my mind and the dark thoughts. Living with Elsie taught me to live outside myself at times. The psychological term is 'disconnection.' I was good at disconnecting. Connecting was too real to for me at different stages in my life. I knew I was intelligent and had a good work ethic. Unfortunately, I was taking on too much stuff. I am amazed I didn't have a breakdown at work or completely lose it with someone. It was a stressful job without all my added pressure. Hadn't I paid my dues? As someone close to me often says "Every form of refuge has its price". It did get to point where the price became too high and I decided to refocus on getting that ever elusive kudo – 'peace'. But this was not the answer for me. Endless judgement and questioning of what I contributed only exacerbated my symptoms of anxiety. I had no choice, but to keep walking this path and find solace somewhere. The fight inside my head was getting worse. I had already opened up the wound, but how was I going to close it?

One day after a session with my therapist I felt particularly anxious when I got home. She had done a role play as to what I would say to the man who assaulted me if he was in the room. I had zoned out as I really didn't want to 'play' that game. When I got home, I was walking around the house in a bit of a daze then there was a loud knock at the door. I looked through the keyhole and when I saw who it was, I just wanted to pretend I wasn't there. I did just that. I went to my son's room and pulled the covers over my head. The loud knocking persisted and persisted, and I begged that if anyone was listening to me to tell him to go away. After a while I had to go and pick my son up from school and they had finally stopped. I was shaking and a bit of a mess. I realised then that I could be triggered to a full-on anxiety attack quite easily at that time. Even so, I carried on as best that I could.

# Strength

Elsie didn't remember everything. She had the patches of memories. I did some desperate things during that time. I wrote letters to people trying to get information. I visited places trying to spark memories and looked at old photos. I became obsessed with getting answers. I thought getting answers would give me closure. But what is closure? Are we ever really rid of a bad memory? The fragments of my brain that were dealing with this were getting tired. I just wanted to sleep and not worry about anything. I was lucky that I had a partner that never gave up on me. No matter how crazy I got. Even so it wasn't pleasant for either of us and I can't believe we are both still standing never mind sane. Life had decided to send a few curly situations to both of us. We used to joke about how many people we must have run over in past lives to be given so many issues to deal with in this life.

# Screaming from my throat

Bringing Elsie's voice to the surface was a slow process. She was stuck in all that cement. Before I knew what was happening to me or my mental health, I remember saying to a friend that I felt like I was 'screaming from my throat'. It felt like I was desperately trying to be heard. Like I was screaming, but my voice could only reach my throat. It could not get to my voice box and come out. I was not generating any sound, but I felt exhausted from screaming anyway. For some time I had been wearing masks to show a very together intelligent and calm woman. In all honesty I felt very panicked and confused inside. Many times, I just wanted to put the covers over my head and forget about everything and anything.

This same friend was very intuitive and said to me quite some time ago, "You are going to write something down one day". I asked what it would be, and she said, "You will know at the time, but it will be important." I believe this is it.

# Moving forward

The timeframe for this process took me around 9 to 10 years. The first two to three years I was confused about what the issues were. I just knew I found it difficult to have a voice. If I had been aware of what was going to happen, I probably would never have begun the journey. Ignorance truly is bliss sometimes. Eventually my screams would dissipate to a loud whine. A three year old not getting her needs met can cause tantrums and stamping feet. This was very embarrassing for a woman in her late 40's. It was going to require a lot of courage to do what was necessary to stop the ache in my throat. I really didn't think I was up to it, but I also underestimated the strength I had inside me. It is amazing how strong someone can become when they get pissed off so many times with bad experiences.

I remember in the days after my Mum passed away, I walked out of the home I was living in after an argument with my partner at the time. I was so disillusioned with the strength life expected me to have. I walked over an hour to a friend's house and along the way there was a gang of young men standing around a car. I thought to myself if they approached me, they would get the wrath of Karen rained upon them. I almost wished they would attempt so I could lay into them and get rid of some anger. Thinking back, it was not the smartest reaction to have. I have had moments in my life when I literally felt like I could move mountains. Inner strength can be very powerful, but if founded on the back of anger clearly unhealthy.

# Blink of an Eye

When I was 34, I was a mother, wife, daughter, sister, and friend. I was doing what was expected in all these roles. Well at least I thought I was. I relied on different people for different things. I probably needed to rely on my own capabilities more. The one person in my life that never faulted with support was my mother. It is a trait that is embedded in your DNA when you start on the journey of motherhood and is never seen as a burden. Support no matter what. Looking back, I had a very similar personality to Mum, although she was probably more outgoing than me. It seems she was also fighting invisible demons that traced back to childhood issues. Even so, she had a heart big enough to help anyone she could.

My aunty and uncle made an impromptu decision to travel from the UK to Perth for a holiday. They had been once before, and my uncle decided on Valentine's Day to come over. It was a lovely surprise for my parents. They spent a week sightseeing and on the 6th Of March went to the local bowling club for a dance. Both my parents and my aunt and uncle certainly knew how to have fun. Dancing away, Mum wearing a pair of her favourite shoes....

I received a phone call from my sister on the Sunday morning saying that Mum had broken her ankle and has been rushed to hospital. Even though Mum had had some small health issues I knew this felt different. I raced down to Fremantle hospital and was greeted by Dad in the carpark. He said she had broken her ankle in two places, and they were going to operate. He told me it wasn't worth going to see her as they were preparing her for surgery. The next day after her surgery my sister and I travelled down to the hospital again to visit her. She was in good spirits and quite jovial, but there was something strange. She hadn't eaten her lunch and she ate anything. She even said she felt strange. I put it down to the after-effects of surgery. The nurse came and said they found something in her blood after doing some tests. My sister and I explained she had an issue with her ankle previously, but they couldn't find what was wrong. I asked them to check with her GP. It seemed to fall on deaf ears.

On the 8th of March 1999 her journey on earth was to end. Abruptly and beyond belief. A few hours after my sister and I had visited her, our mother suffered from a pulmonary embolism. She was 61 years old and still full of life. She was kept on life support till the family could get there and we didn't realise how grim it was till a few hours after getting there. I remember a doctor coming in and I could tell by the look on his face what he was going to say. I felt like I wanted to punch him. I thought if I stop you from saying what you are about to say then it won't be true. Once the words left his mouth they couldn't be taken back. She was brain dead.

My aunty told me she waved to everyone as they closed the ambulance doors at the bowling club. I always like to think that she left this life dancing.

I had a great connection to my Mum

# The Little Things

Her funeral was a real eye-opener for me as she used to joke that no one would turn up. There were many people there. Some people she hadn't seen in a long time. Others were from mine and my sibling's childhood. Several people told me that Mum had helped them, or made a difference in their life without her realising it.

The week leading up to her funeral was a bit of a blur. Anyone who has gone through this phase will tell you that you are moving forward making plans, but you are not really there. You know there is a funeral, but you can still be in denial. My aunty and uncle ended being a great help during that time. Quite a coincidence that they decided to come to Australia very quickly and would end up helping the family in such a personal way.

One night the family was sitting in a circle in Mum and Dad's back room. My brother had been reading up on the afterlife prior to this. We were discussing where we thought she was. There was a spare seat between me and my sister. I was listening to them talking and when I looked up, I saw a figure that looked like Mum enter through the door. (The door was not open). She was wearing her favourite peach coloured top and white cut off pants. She sat in the seat next to me. I remember saying out loud," Mum just walked in." I'm not sure if anyone heard. She looked at me with a very intense sense of peace. I have read about this look in some books. It can feel so peaceful you feel like you will just fall into their face. She didn't say anything, but she gave me two messages. "I am so proud

I created this" (Looking around at the family) and "I am happy you are all talking about this". Then she left. I cannot tell you how she left. I never ever forgot that moment. In fact, it sent me on a lifetime journey of searching for the purpose of life and what is human and what is spirit.

A few months later I spoke to a woman about what I saw. She had been a working medium for some time. She told me to experience anything that involves a spirit presenting themselves to you it would have to happen while you were in an alternative state, or able to access your subconscious. I told her I hadn't slept properly for a few days. I was here but I wasn't (how we all feel when we don't always sleep properly). Sometime later I was talking to a family member who said he saw her. He described what she wore when she walked in. I had not shared that with him and was taken aback at the fact that someone else had seen what I had.

I like to vision my mother left this life dancing

# Becoming Me

Losing Mum so suddenly changed everything for me. It challenged my belief system and sent me on a journey of discovery. This was probably the start of beginning to understand my own journey and why I and basically any human comes to this earth. I started asking a lot of questions and tried to put life into perspective. I stumbled upon spirituality and wanted to know what this all meant. Why the hell do we come here and then just leave? What does this all mean? While searching for answers I have had many wonderful experiences and connected with some beautiful souls. I now realise that my life is much bigger than just my body. My emotions, reactions, physical and mental choices were all part of a bigger picture. I have been asking questions for the past 23 years and even though I haven't found all the answers yet, I am on my way.

Peeling back the layers of who I was would always be a risk for me. I needed to be prepared for what I was going to find underneath. Was I ready for it? I knew once I started, I had to keep going. Like the childhood party game pass the parcel, every now and then I would find a nice surprise. Then I would get frustrated that I was unwrapping and unwrapping and not getting closer to the prize at the end. The prize for me was peace. I just had to define what peace looked like for me.

I wanted to find my purpose and the reason why I was put on this earth. Like a lot of people, I would like my legacy to be somehow leaving this world a better place than when I entered. Wouldn't it be nice for people at my funeral to tell my children I had made a difference in their life like I had been told about my mother?

Becoming emotionally mature can be a very uncomfortable process. It means becoming completely honest with all the good, bad and indifferent parts of who you are. It can be quite confronting to see yourself as others do. I wanted to keep my head high no matter how muddy and distressing things got. People are people and I still had many judgements during this period. Letting go of judgements is a tough one for me. During a self-development course I did, one of the mantras we used was, "What you think of me is none of my business." It is a never ending struggle for me to let go of judgements. I am continually telling myself I am as competent and worthy as anyone, but every now and then something comes at me from left field and my old patterns of thinking come out. Luckily for me I do not stay in the way of thinking anywhere near as much as I used to.

I have dealt with death a few times since Mum's passing, but obviously hers was the most profound. For me to survive my mental anguish and believe there is a purpose to keep fighting I had to find something beyond the physical. Tapping into the parts of me that were not somatic gave me solace that this journey of life was not a waste of time. We truly are spiritual beings having a human experience. But I am still very human and need to fight for my right to be here and my right to be me.

After Mum died, I went on a journey of self-discovery
(On a trip to Kalbarri by myself)

# Surrender

I was affecting the people around me as much as me. It was spilling out and I couldn't contain it anymore. I had to do something. I needed to stop screaming and ask for help and listen. My anger was getting worse, and I could only apologise to people so much. The people close to me understood something was taking hold of me and were forgiving and patient. I had moved to the country and this helped me as I was very comfortable with the surroundings. The bush and ocean were very calming. However, when all my defences were down the truth began to get closer. Looking back anyone would have predicted things were going to come to a crisis point. I had been to counselling so had I learnt strategies to try and understand when I was being triggered. I tried my best to recognise triggers and work on breathing techniques. When I was dealing with more than one thing at a time the walls would come crashing in.

I remember the first time I was triggered and started to get flashbacks. I had an argument with a male adversary. I was so frustrated at his manipulating behaviour. I had no idea at that time how much anger and confusion was manifesting inside of me. When I challenged his behaviour, he turned to me and said, "But Karen I care about you." It was the perfect answer. It made him look good and me look bad in a few words. I felt something shift inside me. It was like a gate had been flung open: a gate that had been contained and locked for years. I started to get visions of a face coming towards me. At that point I could have described him to a police officer to get an identikit picture. The face was a mystery to me. I just knew the feelings attached to the face were very uncomfortable. I felt sick to the stomach when this face came in my head. I wanted to find out the reason why I kept seeing this person. My journey of repressed memories had begun. I was not prepared for what came next. I spent every moment I could to fill in the gaps and get answers. I thought of everyone in my past with that colour hair. I went to hypnotherapy. I spent night after night trying to get to the memories and see who he was and what had happened. Even though I didn't have all the details I knew it was something bad that had happened to me. I knew it was the basis of my fear and anxiety. I knew something in my childhood had been taken away from me. I watched programs on repressed memories. I went back to my childhood home and surrounding areas. I became someone else. She was someone else. That little girl could not have been me. I had a good childhood. I had a normal life. I had good parents and was happy. This happened to someone else. Elsie was created.

# Denial

The only way for me to go forward was to go into denial. That should work, shouldn't it? How wrong was I?

I continued working. I continued on my quest to help people. I was good at my job. I was dedicated and even though it was quite stressful it was important to me to do it properly. I was dealing with anxiety and had been for some time but did not know. I did everything I could to present a strong competent intelligent woman to the world. Actually, that was who I really was. Anxiety can creep up on you. It is closely linked to depression. When it is left to its own devises it can grow without anyone noticing. I could mask my anxiety because I was dedicated to doing a good job.

At the time I worked for an Aged Care and Disability Services Provider. The amount of people that needed help became overwhelming at times. Working in an office also showed its fair share of politics. I was changing and being authentic was becoming very important to me. Whilst working in a zone as a Customer Service Officer I was sitting in a section with my coordinator, assistant coordinator and the CSO manager. I was getting instructions from all three at different times. Of course they all thought I was only doing work for them. I was trying to keep up with the pile of work and noticed that my coordinator had some service plans that were going to be needed to be put into the system. She had not signed off on all of them, but I decided to get a head start by inputting what I could on each one. Then it would not be as much work to do later on. One day my CSO manager sat with me and said the coordinator had asked her to talk to me as she could see that I had put some information in, but I had not finished them. The protocol was after the coordinator gave you the service plans you typed a letter to the client and then got her to approve it all before it was sent out. She said the coordinator had said I didn't know what I was doing. I explained the reasons why I hadn't finished them, because they had not had all the information put in and signed off. I could see the pile was growing so wanted to get a head start on them. I learnt a hard lesson about interfering in a process and helping when someone had not asked. I realised that when you are an outsider you can get blamed for everything that goes wrong. I also learnt that not everyone wants to take responsibility for their actions.

Not long after I asked to be appointed as an office rover which meant I relieved in different sections of the office. Moving around the office was quite unpredictable, but I liked the variety. However, one of the negatives was seeing different sides to all the office politics that were going on. I found it extremely difficult to see so many people hiding behind bullshit. Talking about each other behind their backs and then smiling and encouraging each other in front of their faces. I think part of dealing with symptoms of child abuse is seeing through fake people and manipulation. Paedophiles are very good at grooming and making you feel safe. Adult survivors have a very high bullshit radar. My time at this company was never going to last. I struggle to be around inauthentic people still.

# Never The Right Time

As I kept going forward and stayed happily in denial my energy was spent helping some people around me. We had drama in all sorts of forms. Adolescents pushing boundaries at every opportunity. Sometimes they were pushing boundaries, sometimes I was trying to protect them from boundaries that were being crossed. It was an exhausting sport. I am not going to talk about individual journeys as it is their journeys and stories to tell. For a few years I had embraced meditation and spirituality to keep me from completely going over the edge. I struggled with the material world and the non–material world and tried to balance both. Not an easy task.

I was doing meditation weekly and would write down the messages and insights that came through. One night after a guided meditation the facilitator asked if anyone had thoughts or visions come through. I relayed that I had a vision of a young girl kneeling with a candle flickering a bit away from her. She was praying and, in the distance, there was a gate. All of a sudden the vision was interrupted and someone gave her a perfect shaped peach coloured rose. She held the rose and the edges started to burn. Then a knife came down and chopped the rose and split it in half quite violently. I told the people there it was quite disturbing. The facilitator asked me if I had been through a trauma. The symbols represented innocence of a child and something beautiful being destroyed. It represented innocence being taken away.

Not long after that night my eldest son met a Maori woman who he connected with as they held the same views on spirituality. She was like a mentor to him. He didn't have a room to sleep in at home and was sleeping on the lounge. She offered to rent him a room and it seemed like it was the best solution for everyone at the time. She was quite intuitive and had a passion for healing. She had asked me over to the house to talk about how she saw him fitting in. She didn't want me to think she was taking over a mother role. He was well and truly and adult at this point and didn't need to be mothered. However, he was still quite lost, so he could have benefited from some support.

I felt very comfortable with her and could tell she was very intuitive and had a great interest in healing the world. She had her own health issues but was a fighter. At one point she stopped talking and said suddenly, "I am being told to give you a healing." I never say no to anything that may be of benefit to me. I had experienced Reiki before, but this was different. It was to this day the most profound healing I have ever had. I had tears rolling down my face as it felt so beautiful and raw. When I got up I said to her that was very intense. She had a strained look on her face. She said to me "I am going to ask you something." Were you sexually abused when you were very young?" I was stunned. I felt shame and relief both at once. I collapsed into her. She said to come and sit down. She said Mum had told her it was time. It was time for me to understand my life. I was a bit confused why Mum would be saying that. I asked if Mum knew about what happened to me. She said she was aware something happened, but didn't know all the details. Mum had spoken to some friends concerned something may have happened to me. She was told by more than one person that I was too young to remember and would forget.

Growing up Mum was very protective of me. Knowing something had happened to me after I went missing was something that gnawed at her. I have a vivid memory of being dropped off at our house by a lovely couple. Mum came running out of the house to greet the car. I don't know the time frame I was missing. It could have been one hour it could have been a few hours. I know it wasn't all day. Even though her friends said I wouldn't remember, she couldn't let that guilt go. She didn't share anything with my father because she was worried about his reaction to her and the thought that something had happened to me. My father was a black belt in Karate, and would not have let things go without finding who did it. She hoped, as her friends suggested that the kindest scenario would be that I wouldn't remember, and all would be fine. Trying to get something out of me would confuse me and make things worse. Three year old children don't remember everything anyway. I certainly don't blame her for that or anything else.

Ruby, (The Maori woman) told me that I needed to get counselling. I asked her to tell me what she saw but she refused and again said I needed to get counselling. I told her I was aware that something had happened. Accessing my subconscious had been overtaking me in the last few years. I talked about a time when I was 6 or 7. She stopped me and said no you were 3. These are separate instances. She continued to say the person was known to the family, but distant to them. She said my world was going to get very dark while I was dealing with this. I went and saw her again, but she would never tell me what she saw. I found another hypnotherapist in Joondalup who I trusted straight away. She was able to take me back to some memories and I wrote down the things I recounted. I was in my lounge room when a memory came to me which I wrote down. I saw myself as a 3 year old. Even though I was watching the memory I felt like I was there and felt every bit of the fear and anguish. I wrote a letter to myself with the memory which I keep in a safe place. My hypnotherapist referred me to a psychologist who I saw for two and a half years. My partner and I had made the decision to move to the country so I finished the sessions with my psychologist. I felt comfortable that I had made headway, but I didn't realise that I had not really faced my real issues. This was to happen a few years later.

# R U OK?

In 2016 I went to Thailand to visit my son who had been ordained as a monk the year before. He lived at a monastery in the mountains of the Udon Thani Province. I was aware of what to expect staying at the monastery as my partner and I had visited the year before when he was ordained. Because I was on my own and a westerner, I got a lot more attention this time. I found myself feeling quite overwhelmed. Again, I did not recognise that I had symptoms of anxiety. After leaving the monastery I had my credit card taken at an ATM and the battery on my mobile phone burnt out. I stepped through each problem and worked it out, but by the time I got home I was highly stressed and my symptoms were getting worse. I went to my GP for a check and she took my blood pressure. She said that my blood pressure was extremely high. She could put me on tablets, or I could find healthy ways to get my blood pressure down. This was a bit if a wakeup call for me. Mum had died in her early 60's and I wanted to be around for my family longer than 52. I decided I needed to change my lifestyle. Unfortunately, I didn't get help quickly enough and started to jeopardise the relationships around me. I basically had a mini breakdown.

I heard a story about a woman who ended her marriage after having a fight about the vegemite jar lid being left off. Obviously, there was more to it. She felt unheard about a lot of stuff. She had told her husband it annoyed her when he just left the vegemite jar lid off and didn't bother putting it away. She had told him this many times. Not being heard builds up and one day you shout loudly.

I was watching television one day and it was R U OK Day. I was posting messages on Facebook and checking in with my friends. I listened to an Australian Celebrity's account of when he realised he had an anxiety disorder. I realised *I wasn't* **OK**.

I had even found driving hard and going to the shops was very uncomfortable for me as there were so many people. It felt like I was starting to get symptoms of agoraphobia. One day I was stopped by a stranger at a local shopping centre to ask me if I was alright. I must have had a distant look on my face. I had to reach out. I found a program run by Macquarie University that did courses on Cognitive Behavioural Therapy. I did a test with them and scored severely on the Social Anxiety Disorder scale and scored in every anxiety disorder except OCD. The hardest part for me was acknowledgement. Acknowledgement that had I had been struggling for years. I sent an email to my family telling them I was going to do the CBT course and that I had been fighting an anxiety disorder for some years. Just acknowledging it was huge for me. I was afraid that by admitting I had a mental illness I would be seen as dumb or incompetent. I was an intelligent person that was capable of making decisions. I still believe there is a stigma against mental illness. I started exercising 3 times week and went to a yoga class once a week. I decided to do the 8 week course on CBT. My blood pressure started to come down and I became hopeful that I could work on my symptoms and look forward to a bright future.

# Stepping Out of Denial

Part of coming out of denial was speaking to people about what I was going through. When I had emailed people close to me about my decision to do Congenital Behavioural Therapy (CBT) I didn't tell them why. That was to come. It took a lot of courage to admit I needed help because it felt like I was admitting that I was a bit crazy. That would have to mean I wasn't intelligent. Dealing with mental illness has nothing to do with your intelligence, but I couldn't help but feel some people would think I was dumb.

The only way for me to get better was to say I needed help, so I took a deep breath and dove in. Being listened to was very important because I had been silent for so long.

I wanted to write down my thoughts and was told to write a book. When I told my partner about this, he said to be careful. He told me I needed to protect the innocent. I said straight back, *"I am the innocent."* I have spent a lot of time to worrying about protecting people and concerned about judgements I may get. I did this at the detriment of my own mental health.

# No Guarantees- Bravery.

I plucked up the courage to go and speak to my father. I told him that I wanted my family to understand me better. There was a reason why my life had become so chaotic. This was not a question of blame for anyone. It was a plea to be understood. I never imagined I would be brave enough to talk to Dad. It felt like a huge weight had been taken off me once I did. Dad never once said he didn't believe me. In fact, he was quite concerned I had been through all of that on my own. I told him It was the 1960's. Stuff happened. It was a lot different to today.

Dad lived in England during the second world war. He didn't sleep in his own bed for years as they would go to a bunker and take cover against potential bombings. To this day certain sounds trigger his memories. Memories of houses being bombed and then finding out the next day which houses and who had survived. He recalls being told of a man that had been killed was the man who had played the part of Santa Clause for the children at Christmas. Pretty sad for a kid to hear Santa Clause had died. Death may have been a bit more acceptable during that time, but still not OK and frightening. The night my Great Grandfather passed away my dad was put in the same room as his dead Grandfather as there was nowhere else to sleep that night.

When I told him what I remembered (edited) he was shaken and said, "But we all went through that together. Of course it was bad, but we had each other. You went through this on your own."

I have never blamed my parents at all. Even though Mum may have known something happened I am not sure there was anything she could have done to make things different. I was on the cusp of forming my memories and bringing out such a bad situation then would not have helped me. Talking to Dad was very empowering to me. I felt quite relieved.

Each generation throughout history has its own version of trauma. Trauma resides in the individual. Being trapped in a cycle is hell on earth. Having a voice can penetrate the wall of hell. Reaching out to listen can bring the person back to life. Life here on earth. Life as a human with all the privileges that brings. The happiness that can bring, but most of all the love and connection that brings.

I started to unravel the anxiety symptoms and began to control them a lot more. I was not fully over them and still had a small part of me that I felt was not being heard.

# Me Too

There has been a lot of historical abuse cases come to the surface in recent years. I started seeing the likes of Rolf Harris and Robert Hughes being exposed as paedophiles and coming to justice. It continued to stir the unheard voice inside me. I saw the sense of relief on the people they had affected. I continued to believe that being heard was just not possible for me. There was a couple of people I had shared stuff with. It wasn't fair to offload on one or two people that couldn't really help me. It was selfish to get relief and I still wanted to hide.

I was reading a profile of a friend of mind on Facebook. The lady is an art therapist and she spoke freely for the 'Me Too' movement that was started by Tarana Burke. It was highlighted again by Rose McGowan in 2017. Rose had been abused by Harvey Weinstein and once she made the choice to come out with what happened it had a flow on effect that was definitely not expected. I messaged my friend and told her how brave it was of her to write her story to give others the freedom to write theirs. I explained I did not feel comfortable talking about anything on a public forum. I asked her if I could come and see her privately and see what we could do to bring my story to the surface.

She helped to express Elsie's voice in art. I still have the painting and have showed some people. I went to see her a few times and started to feel quite empowered. I had written a letter to my sister the year before but did not have the courage to send it. There was no turning back if I sent that letter. I created a diary and kept the letter in the front in an envelope. I went away camping with my partner and took the diary with me. One day I told him I was sending the letter. I am not sure he understood fully the courage it took. I finally was at the stage that being heard was not as important as having a voice and asking for understanding. I sent the letter and never expected a reply.

A week or two later I received a simple card with two teddy bears on the front. One was a little bigger than the other and was hugging the smaller one. Inside she acknowledged my voice.

It was amazing how much healing I received from that. I am trying to get on with my life. I don't want to continually make this about me. Although I would like to come out of hiding for other people's sake.

The card my sister sent me gave me a lot of healing.

# Forgiveness

He came to me in a dream before I went to therapy. He was in a jail setting and he had shorter hair. He said sorry. He said he didn't realise how much it affected my life and that he had issues with his own childhood abuse -especially from his mother. Growing up he had struggled with low self-esteem issues. He flexed his muscles and asked me if I thought he was good looking. He was looking for forgiveness...

Some people say paedophiles have a disease that cannot be cured. If that is true then there needs to be a lot more research into this as there is in in other incurable diseases. Why do these people come to earth to make their life and the lives of so many children a misery? Is this the Universe's sick joke? "I'm sending these people to earth so just deal with them and live with it."

It is not a natural state for human beings to hurt. It is a natural state to give love and feel love. Anything beyond that is not human. I heard a saying the other day, "You only have to forgive once. It's the resentment you live with." (Cianfrance, D, "et al", 2017). This is what I am dealing with. So, do I forgive him? Yes, I forgave him some time ago. Not for his sake for mine. He has to forgive himself. I know I was not the only one he molested. Forgiving himself is his process.

I also forgave my parents for not knowing or understanding, but I have still been living with the resentment. Resentment of not having a voice, of stifling my courage and of being crippled with fear at the littlest of things. Whenever something seemed hard or scary, I would run. But most of all, the resentment of not being who I was supposed to be. I have always imagined my younger, confident self running barefoot and wearing sunflowers in my hair. Dancing, painting and having the freedom to just be me. Sometimes I use the sunflower as a symbol when I want to tap into the unique, confident me.

# It Doesn't Belong to You

Intimacy is a sacred thing. Giving yourself to someone is giving them all your vulnerability. Giving them your shame and trusting them with it. When an adult forces a sexual act upon a child whether it is an inappropriate touch or God forbid the worst most violent act, they take away their identity. They take away something that was never given to them They take away who that person was supposed to be. When a child has their identity taken away, they search their whole lives looking for themselves. I hid inside myself and coming out was very scary. I trusted the world at 3 years old and felt very safe. This person destroyed my trust in anyone around me and I spent a lot of time in flight or fight mode. That chronic state can change anyone.

A child has no concept of sexual acts or the connection they have to their body. So when you use a child's body you take away part of their soul. Then they end up spending the rest of their lives searching for it.

I felt a lot of shame about my behaviour over time. I felt shame about the fear I held in and definitely felt the shame of not being able to control my anger. I still struggle with body image. When I was very young I only used to draw heads of people and not the body. I still do that sometimes today. But this process for me has made me a better person. We are all so much more than just a body. It is our mind and spirit that makes us who we are.

Being accountable for your actions is important. Then let it go.

As long as you don't cause harm to anyone you can forgive yourself. You can't force others to forgive you. I cannot dwell in shame as I have to be kind to myself and move forward. I have a lot to give to this world.

# Forgiving Her

A good friend of mine pointed out to me that as much work as I have done on myself, I have not fully connected with my inner child. Having the ability to separate her by calling her someone else I also was able to dislike her and disconnect from the part that makes me whole. My next step is to connect to my inner child and embrace her for who she is and who she made me. I had a moment not long ago when I was listening to a song in the car and was really enjoying it. I imagined dancing and my grandfather was there. I invited my inner child to dance. As I did, I got very emotional. I danced with her for a short while. Then I visioned my grandfather holding her on his hip and the three of us dancing together. Inviting my inner child to have fun with me is very important. It will get easier and easier. I have had some wonderful experiences in my life and choose to focus on those. I know have many more wonderful experiences to come.

Elsie is no longer someone else. She is part of me. Every part of me. She made me who I am today.

# Ending (not quite.......)

Memory repression is very misunderstood and can happen to anyone. There is still a stigma attached to this subject and there needs to be more research done and more help available for people going through it.

"When confronted with trauma a child may not have the ability to cope with the experience. While every young child may not remember specific events, they do remember emotions, images, and can be reminded of situations that cause them to be upset." (kidsmentalhealthinfo.com, n.d.)

I spent a long time looking for external proof even though I had all the symptoms and internal proof. Usually, proof comes after you need it. A lot of the time the perpetrator is old or dead. It can be a very cruel process trying to heal from something that does not have a substance like a real memory does. I wondered what would happen if I ever found him. I am actually grateful I didn't.

CBT helped me to retrain my brain to not always go immediately into fight or flight mode when triggered. I recommend it to anyone struggling. Finding and connecting to my inner child is going to help me to have the confidence to step into who I truly am.

# References

Brown, Brene, 2010, The *Power of Vulnerability*, 12/04/2022 https://www.youtube.com/watch?v=iCvmsMzlF7o

Cianfrance, D., Heyman, D., Clifford, J., In Patane, R., In Helton, J., Desplat, A., Arkapaw, A., ... Heyday Films,. (2017). *The light between oceans*.

**Chicago** (Author–Date, 15<sup>th</sup> ed.)

Peterson, Carole, 2017 *Childhood Amnesia in Children: A Prospective Study Across Eight Years,10/10/2021,* https://srcd.onlinelibrary.wiley.com/doi/abs/10.1111/cdev.12972

*Young children remember traumatic events* n.d. https://www.kidsmentalhealthinfo.com/faq/young-children-remember-traumatic-events